DUBLIN BUSES

RICHARD WALTER

AMBERLEY

Front cover: Go-Ahead Wright Gemini 11565 (182-D-474) is seen climbing out of the coastal suburb of Dun Laoghaire on route 59 to Killiney Hill.

Rear cover: Dublin Bus has used several different City Tour liveries. The current Do Dublin tour livery is worn by open-topper AV93.

First published 2020

Amberley Publishing
The Hill, Stroud
Gloucestershire, GL5 4EP

www.amberley-books.com

Copyright © Richard Walter, 2020

The right of Richard Walter to be identified as the Author of this work has been asserted in accordance with the Copyrights, Designs and Patents Act 1988.

ISBN 978 1 4456 9195 4 (print)
ISBN 978 1 4456 9196 1 (ebook)

British Library Cataloguing in Publication Data.
A catalogue record for this book is available from the British Library.

Typesetting by Aura Technology and Software Services, India. Printed in UK.

Contents

Introduction

Although I live near Edinburgh and have a specific interest in all things to do with buses in the UK, I have always been fascinated by public transport in Ireland, and in particular in Dublin itself.

Back in 2007, to mark the twentieth anniversary of Dublin Bus (Bus Átha Cliath), Jonathan McDonnell, Darren Hall and Ian Molloy wrote the fascinating and beautifully illustrated book *Dublin Bus – Changing with the City 1987–2006* (Ian Allan Publishing). I started taking photographs in Dublin around about 2006 and have made many visits in the subsequent years to catch up with developments. So I hope that readers might find this book interesting as it picks up what has happened since the original book, although I would stress that it is nowhere as detailed. I am particularly pleased, however, to have had one of the authors of that book, Darren Hall, contribute to this little piece.

Dublin Buses was formed back in February 1987, when services were split out of the Córas Iompair Éireann (CIE), and has in time become a modern and forward-thinking bus operator. The livery on the main bus fleet has changed significantly over the years. There have also been white wedding buses, an assortment of liveries for the airport service and some colourful variations of City Tour liveries. The centre of Dublin is a showcase for many types of buses and other operators too and is a great place to find good vantage points for photographs with some attractive and impressive backdrops.

During July 2018, plans were revealed for a complete overhaul of Dublin's bus services. The changes planned by the National Transport Authority have led to a renumbering of key routes and changes and improvements to frequencies. One of the biggest changes has seen the arrival of the Go-Ahead company in Dublin. As this book goes to press, there are still changes to come and it is likely that there will be many more developments in 2020 and beyond.

For this book I wanted to capture how the company has continued to develop over the last ten years or so and illustrate some of the unique vehicle types which have seen service in the city. I have also included a section covering some of the open and closed top tours of Dublin which have seen some changes in operator and liveries in recent years.

If you haven't visited Dublin, or been there for a while, I would warmly recommend a trip to sample the many types of buses around, as well as the beautiful city of course. You won't be disappointed.

My grateful thanks go to local experts Darren Hall and Noel O'Rawe for their much-appreciated contributions and assistance, and to Andrew Chalmers, Donald MacRae, Thomas McReynolds and Alistair Train for helping in filling gaps for some of the buses that I missed. All are credited for their particular work. The uncredited pictures were taken by myself.

EV94 (08-D-30064) – one of two ADL E400-bodied Volvo B7TLs in Dublin Pride 2019 livery – the theme being the fiftieth anniversary of the Stonewall riots and the evolution of gay rights in Ireland. A photo of the other bus, EV98, is on page 23. (Darren Hall)

The Single-Deckers

Alexander Setanta Volvo B10B AD 62 (94-D-33062) is one of a batch of dual-door vehicles delivered to Dublin Bus between 1993 and 1995. It is seen out of service, resting between duties.

Low-floor Wright Volvo B6BLEs featured wheelchair accessible technology. WV20 (99-D-60020) is seen on the 53 to the city centre. The bus subsequently became a shuttle bus with Bewleys Hotel at Dublin airport.

WV29 (00-D-70029) was a Wright Crusader II Volvo B6BLE and was photographed on service 123 to Marino.

Dublin Bus was keen to operate articulated buses. One example was Wright Eclipse Fusion-bodied Volvo B7LA AW9 (00-D-65009), seen on route 4 to St Vincent's Hospital.

Another example shown here is AW3 (00-D-65003), also on service 4 to Monkston Avenue. This bus was one of a very small number to see further service in the UK where it became X961 CNO.

Representing a more modern single-deck vehicle with Dublin Bus is Wright Streetlite W52 (172-D-22742), which was caught starting a service 59 to Killiney Hill at Dun Laoghaire.

With the magnificent harbour of Dun Laoghaire in the background, this is another view of W52 (172-D-22742) on the 59 to Killiney Hill.

Leyland and Volvo Olympians

Volvo Olympian RV468 (99-D-468) is seen in the attractive City Swift network livery on service 42B to Blundern Drive in Coolock.

Leyland Olympian RH31 (90-D-1031), which was later to become one of the company's Ghost Buses, in O'Connell Street on service 19 to Bulfirn Road. Just visible above the lower windows is route branding. (Donald MacRae)

Volvo Olympian RH530 (99-D-10530) was later to become Lords of Kingston T915 EGD after it left Dublin Bus. It is seen carrying out duties on service 15B to Whitechurch Estate.

Volvo Olympian RA197 (95-D-197) was out of service when this photograph was taken. It was to later become a driver training vehicle in the fleet. It is testament to the quality of these buses that so many went on to see further use after withdrawal.

Another example of a Volvo Olympian: RV343 (97-D-343) operating the 78A to Liffey Valley Centre. The bus ended up in the UK as an open-top bus on City Sightseeing Bristol duties.

This rather shocking and severe all-over vinyl-wrapped Volvo Olympian, RV433 (98-D-204330), with 'No Nonsense Car Insurance' advertising was in service with AMC coaches before becoming Express Bus where it wore a wrap for the National Aquatic Centre in Blanchardstown.

Originally new to Dublin Bus as RV564 (99-D-564), this Volvo Olympian is now in service with Barton's of Maynooth and is regularly seen performing cruise ship transfers. Many cruise ships come into Dublin and shuttle work is much in demand from local bus and coach operators.

Beechfield Coaches operates a large number of coaches and buses for contract work and private hire in Dublin. Former Dublin Bus Volvo Olympian RV 466 (99-D-466), in a very distinctive green livery, was pictured on a school contract in the centre of the city.

Another example of new work for a former Dublin Bus Volvo Olympian is RV480 (99-D-480), which now operates with Kelly Coaches.

Former Dublin Bus RV620 (99-D-620), pictured with current owner Barton's of Maynooth.

A breakdown wagon in operation with an Olympian about to be towed from Parnell Square.

Alexander ALX400 and Transbus Trident 2 Volvo B7TLs

Dublin Bus received a sizeable number of Alexander ALX400-bodied Volvo B7TLs between 2000 and 2006. An early example is AV287 (03-D-20287). Buses from AV186 upwards featured a more curved version, not unlike those on the previous RH/RA/RV Class.

AV324 (03-D-20324), on the 145 to Kilmacanogue, shows the earlier style of windscreen fitted.

Newly built AX469 (06-D-30469) was pictured when leaving the Alexanders factory at Falkirk in 2006. (Thomas McReynolds)

AV69 (00-D-40069) on the 11 to Kilmacud. The bus spent most of its working life at Donnybrook depot but transferred to Phibsboro for a short time and spent its final three weeks of operation at Summerhill.

Showing the original Transport for Ireland logo, AX524 (06-D-30524) is seen on the popular 46A service to Dun Laoghaire.

Heading over the O'Connell Bridge, this is AV324 (02-D-20324) on service 54A to Kiltipper.

AX640 (06-D-30640) is seen entering service from the terminus at Dun Laoghaire.

On its way into Dun Laoghaire on service 75 is AX639 (06-D-30639). This is one of the routes that was taken over by Go-Ahead Ireland during 2018.

AV385 (04-D-20385) passes along Custom House Quay on service 15 to Ringsend Road.

An oddity in the Dublin Buses ancillary fleet is converted Alexander ALX Volvo B7TL AV144 (00-D-70144). It performs tree-lopping duties, as have other vehicles in the past. Such a vehicle is not a familiar sight elsewhere. (Noel O'Rawe)

A number of vehicles in the Dublin Bus fleet have carried all-over advertising – traditionally hand-painted but now using vinyls. AV397 (04-D-20397), in an all-over wrap for HB Ice Cream, turns from Eden Quay on the 54A to Kiltripper. HB Ice Cream is a brand in Ireland which is part of the Unilever Group's Heartbrand range. (Noel O'Rawe)

AV415 (05-D-10415) is advertising Coca-Cola when photographed on College Street on the 15C to Rossmore. (Noel O'Rawe)

Film advertising has become very popular on public transport. AX469 (06-D-30469) promotes the James Bond film *Skyfall* and was seen out of service on Pearse Street. (Noel O'Rawe)

Fashion is also promoted by bus advertising. AX582 (06-D-30582) is wrapped for PrettyLittleThing.com ('Your one-stop shop for trend-led women's clothing at seriously killer prices') and sits in Blanchardstown Centre on the 39 to Ongar. (Noel O'Rawe)

In 2017, Dublin Bus management, in discussions with staff from minority groups, decided to become more involved with the Pride movement. Donnybrook-based AX523 was the first bus to be so treated. (Darren Hall)

AX646 is seen in a subsequent version of the Pride Bus in 2018. The 'Proud Dads' is a reference to Dublin Bus staff whose children are part of the LGBTQ community. It is seen on an evening service on route 7 to Brides Glen on O'Connell Street. (Darren Hall)

Dublin Bus supported the Dublin Pride Festival for 2018 with two ¾ wraps, including AX647 and AX488 Volvo B7TL/ALX400. AX647 is seen in Kiltipper, Tallaght on service 54A. (Darren Hall)

EV98 is the other of the two ADL E400-bodied Volvo B7TLs in Dublin Pride 2019 rainbow colours. A photo of EV64 is on page 5. (Darren Hall)

Dublin Bus has adapted a distinctive white and red livery for its dedicated driver training fleet. An example is Transbus Alexander Volvo B7LDD AV46 (00-D-40046).

Another example of the driver training fleet is AV85 (00-D-40085). (Alistair Train)

Former Dublin Bus AV354 (03-D-50354) was acquired by P. J. Dignan & Son of Athy, County Kildare, and is seen on cruise line duties.

Representing one of the Dublin Bus DT Class Transbus Trident 2 ALX400s is former DT10 (03-D-10010), which is now operating with Ashbourne Connect. The last day of DT operation in Dublin was 12 December 2017.

Former Dublin Bus AV329 (03-D-20329) is seen on a Princess Cruises shuttle service owned by Dublin Coaches.

This vehicle was new as AV5 (00-D-4005) and is now running with Barton's Coaches.

Alexander Dennis Enviro ALX500s

Dublin Bus bought a number of tri-axle Alexander Dennis Enviro 500 Volvo D9A-300/Volvo D9B-310s between 2005 and 2007. This photo shows one of the 2007 batch just after completion at the Alexander Dennis factory in Falkirk, Scotland. (Thomas McReynolds)

Straight off the production line, VT23 (07-D-70023) leaves Alexander's, Falkirk, on 18 July 2007. (Thomas McReynolds)

Seen early on a very sunny morning, VT37 (07-D-70037) is on the 25X Xpresso service to Belfield.

VT19 (05-D-70019) approaching the 46A terminus at Dun Laoghaire.

Showing off the unique shaped side ads applied to nearsides as well as offsides, VT08 (05-D-70008) is running not on service in central Dublin.

VT12 (05-D-70012) shows the effect of the large nearside advert full-on.

VT20 (05-D-70020) heads into central Dublin on the busy service 46A to Phoenix Park. This route was dominated by the tri-axles for a number of years. (Alistair Train)

Another view at Dun Laoghaire on a rather wet and miserable day. VT5 (05-D-7005) has a special advert promoting taxsaver, which could allow passengers a 52 per cent savings on their commute.

VT4 (05-D-70004) is on Marine Road at Dun Laoghaire on the 75 to The Square.

Showing the latest Transport for Ireland (TFI) logos, VT70 (07-D-70070) is on the 39A to UCD Belfield. It is numerically the last of the VT Class.

Alexander Enviro400s

This unidentified brand-new Enviro400 was photographed at Cardonald while on delivery to Dublin Bus on 8 July 2007. (Thomas McReynolds)

Fully liveried new EV17 (07-D-30017) was also pictured at Cardonald on 8 July 2007. (Thomas McReynolds)

EV02 (07-D-30002) leaving Alexander's at Falkirk on 8 July 2007. (Thomas McReynolds)

An early morning sunny view of EV95 (08-D-30095) on the service 145 to Kilmacanogue.

Pictured on a diversion, EV34 (07-D-30034) is on service 155, which operates to the Ikea store.

The very distinctive shape of the Enviro400 is noticeable in this photo of EV40 (07-D 30040) on the 123 to Kilnamangh Road.

EV97 (08-D-30097) in fleet livery and EV49 (07-D-30049), newly converted to open top for the Do Dublin tour fleet, passing the company HQ on O'Connell Street.

EV40 (07-D-30064) heads a line-up of buses at Dublin Airport on a very rainy afternoon, setting off for Balinteer on the 16.

EV64 (08-D-30064) operating on the 40 to Liffey Valley in Wedding Bus livery.

EV100 (08-D-30100) in an over-all vinyl wrap for Carroll's New York Deli.

Wright Gemini Volvos

Dublin Bus has taken delivery of a large number of Wright Gemini-bodied Volvo B9TL and B5TLs since 2007. With Wrightbus going into administration in September 2019, it is unclear if there will ever be any more buses from this well-known bodybuilder. SG163 (161-D-39452) turns into Parnell showing a 'Not in Service' digital screen.

Putting off time in the city is SG178 (161-D-43824), having completed its journey on the 40B.

A friendly wave from the driver as GT97 (132-D-6201) heads off from Dun Laoghaire on a 46A to Phoenix Park.

GT88 (132-D-1724) crosses O'Connell Street on a 46E to Mountjoy Square.

SG115 (152-D-14668) picks up passengers on Marine Road in Dun Laoghaire on the 7A to Loughlinston Park.

SG523 (191-D-4613) heads through Parnell Street on a 40 to Charlestown.

Seen on Westmoreland Street is SG290 (172-D-17845), operating a service 37 to Blanchardstown.

GT125 is seen in a wrap for 'St Helens in Adamstown', a planned town in West Dublin. This bus is now numbered 11907 with Go-Ahead Ireland, based at their Ballymount Depot. (Darren Hall)

There are other Wright Geminis that have appeared in Dublin which were not initially new to Dublin Bus. 03-D-121563 would appear to originate from London, if the traces of red are an indication, and is seen operating Parkwest Route 860 for Express of Mulhuddart.

Many buses from the UK end up in Ireland. DD19 (03-D-121565) is an ex-London Arriva Wrightbus Volvo B7TL, VLW 187 (LJ03 MKM), and is displaying a board saying that it is bound for Parkwest on Route 860. The identity of the current owner (Express of Mulhuddart) is not made clear. The covered windows seem somewhat extreme.

Dedicated Airport Buses

Dublin International Airport has benefitted from frequent bus links into the city. Alexander-bodied ALX400 V118 (00-D-70118) shows off one of the original dedicated airport liveries.

AV128 (00-D-70128) carries the now familiar and attractive two-tone green Airlink livery. The Airlink Express offers two routes. The 747 operates from the airport to Dublin's main bus station (Busaras) and then via O'Connell Street to Heuston train station. The 757 route runs from the airport to Camden (Charlotte Way and Harcourt Street).

Representing the current vehicles operated on the Airlink Express is VG42 (09-D-2135). The two routes connect with the Central Bus Station (as seen in the photograph) and many of the city's railway stations as well as services on the Dublin Bus public transport network.

VG41 (09-D-213), featuring window fare branding. This has since been removed.

Screened up out of service as it arrives at Dublin airport, this is VG44 (09-D-2138).

VG34 (09-D-2123) carries full Airlink Express livery but has no branding.

Dublin Bus Tour Vehicles

Dublin is a popular tourist destination and offers a number of choices for tours of the city and beyond. Dublin Bus has been very active in providing quality services. Volvo Olympian RA218 (95-D-218) shows one of the early liveries and City Tours branding in a sunny O'Connell Street.

Closed-top Alexander ALX400 Volvo B7TL AV257 (02-D-10257) operated the company's Coastal Tour and is seen at the departure point in O'Connell Street.

Volvo Olympian RA217 (95-D-217) rests between tours. Two types of semi open-top layout can be seen when you compare it to the bus behind.

Pictured in a subsequent livery and rebranded as the Dublin Bus Tour, Volvo Olympian RA218 (95-D-218) is seen before entering its day's service. The live commentaries were a joy to listen to. Each driver had his own personal stories and jokes to add to the tour scripts and no two journeys were the same.

Leyland Olympian RH67 (91-D-1067) is pictured on a hotel pick-up shuttle service which took residents to the formal starting point of the Dublin Bus Tour.

Volvo B7TL AV93 (00-D-40093) with a full load of passengers on the hop-on, hop-off tour.

Volvo B7TL AV179 (00-D-70179) loading up at the O'Connell Street pick-up point.

Pictured at Dun Laoghaire is closed-top Volvo B7TL AV398 (04-D-20398) in Coastal Tour livery.

AX496 (06-D30496) arrives at Dublin's main bus station, showing off a completely revised tour livery under the DoDublin banner.

Out of service AX512 (06-D-30512) and a colourful selection of buses in O'Connell Street.

DoDublin open-top AX441 is seen in a full wrap for Dublin Pride 2019 – the only open-top to be so treated. It is seen near Kilmainham Gaol. (Darren Hall)

Proving that semi open-toppers are popular on rainy days is the reasonably well loaded AX496 (06-D-30496).

EV50 (07-D-30050). 2019 was the thirty year anniversary of Dublin Bus. As well as publicising the occasion on the DoDublin tour buses, the vehicle shows that City Sightseeing tickets are accepted.

EV50 (07-D-30050) is seen in Parnell Square by the Dublin Writers Museum.

AX542 (06-02-30542) in From Gardens to Mountains branding.

AX544 (06-D-30544) at O'Connell Bridge in the very attractive and eye-catching 'The 1916 Tour' livery. It is now a promotional vehicle with 98FM radio station but is still owned by Dublin Bus. (Noel O'Rowe)

Ghost Bus *Molly* DF450 (450-ZD). Dublin Buses has operated a Ghostbus tour for some years, playing on the fact that Bram Stoker, who wrote *Dracula*, was born in Dublin. The bus is a DAF DK 1160 engined Leyland Atlantean PDR1A/1 with Metal Sections Limited Bodywork assembled by CIE at their factory in Dublin. (Donald MacRae)

DF450 (450-ZD) was operated as the sole Ghostbus until 2006, when she started to get a little creaky! RH31 was then converted due to the popularity of the tour. (Donald MacRae)

Leyland Olympian RH31 (90-D-1031) became *Molly 2* in the Ghostbus fleet of Dublin Bus. (Donald MacRae)

Another view of the second Ghostbus *Molly*, RH31, which (as with the original) proved to be a very popular attraction. (Donald MacRae)

ALX400/Volvo B7TL AV63 (00-D-40063), named *Lucy* after a character from Bram Stoker's *Dracula*, is one of two current Ghostbuses based at Summerhill Garage and used on the nocturnal ghost bus service. It is seen in the daylight on a publicity/promo service in June 2014. (Darren Hall)

The other current vehicle used, AV64, is called *Mina* (00-D-40064) and is also a converted ALX400/Volvo B7TL which features maze-like corridors leading up to 'a stark Victorian theatre complete with red blood curtains'.

Other Operators' Tours of Dublin

Formerly with Dublin Bus as RH103, Alexander RH Olympian (91-D-10103) passed to the operator Dualway and is seen in the original distinctive yellow livery for its tour of Dublin.

Another of the same batch is former RH104 (91-D-10104), seen on O'Connell Street.

Dualway became part of the City Sightseeing franchise and Alexander Leyland Olympian RH132 (92-D-132) wore this red front to reflect this. The bus was, sadly, burnt out in a fire at the Dualway depot in April 2011.

The full and final City Sightseeing livery is shown on Dualway former Dublin Bus Alexander ALX Volvo B7TL AV100 (00-D-40100).

The London AEC Routemaster gets around. Examples appear all over the world. Former RMA25 (67-D-813) was operated by Dualway, initially in a brown and cream livery before receiving the City Sightseeing branding.

Former London General AEC Routemaster RML2729 (SMK 729F) became ZV 7699 in the Dualway Coaches fleet.

Independent operator McConn operated this East Lancs Scania, 99-D-28988, on the Gray Line Dublin Bay and Castle tour and it carried Coca-Cola branding.

Dualway operated former Dublin Bus Alexander Leyland Olympian RH59 (90-D-1059) with 'Irish City Tours' logo.

Dualway vehicles carried a number of variations of City Sightseeing livery. Former Dublin Bus Alexander Leyland Olympian RH11 (90-D-1011) is pictured approaching the city centre.

Dualway East Lancs Vyking-bodied Volvo B7TL 04-D-40940 is seen showing a minimal application of City Sightseeing lettering.

Sporting a large pint of Guinness on its side is Alexander ALX Volvo B7TL, new to Dublin Bus as AV227 (01-D-10227).

Another example of an East Lancs-bodied Volvo B7TL, this is Dualway 05-D-28639.

Volvo Olympian 98-D-77635 came to Dualway from London United, where it was numbered VA42 and registered R942 YOV. Its livery is partially obscured by an offside advert.

Shown in the attractive grounds of Phoenix Park is Dualway former Dublin Bus Alexander Volvo Olympian RH501 (99-D-501).

Taking a break between tours is Dualway 92-D-134 – previously RH134 with Dublin Bus.

Pictured on the Dualway red tour is 00-D-70135 – formerly Dublin Bus Alexander ALX Volvo B7TL AV135.

Also operating a Dualway red tour is Mylennium Nordic 07-D-29.

Promoting the Dublin City by Night tour is Dualway 03-D-82308. It was formerly Go-Ahead London Central Plaxton President PVL361 (PJ53 NKF).

Dualway Transbus Plaxton-bodied Volvo B7TL 03-D-120284 is seen in a different City Sightseeing livery. It was originally PVL360 (PJ53 NKE) with Go-Ahead London Central.

10-D-6224 is a Visionaire Volvo B9TL that was delivered new to Dualway and is seen in Phoenix Park.

Dualway Alexander ALX400 Volvo B7TL 00-D-40095, which was new to Dublin Bus as AV95.

Dualway Alexander ALX400 Volvo B7TL 00-D-40072, also new to Dublin Bus as AV72.

Dualway Myllenium Nordic 07-D-29, displaying 'Hop-On Hop-Off' clearly on its digital screen.

Dualway Alexander ALX400 Volvo B7TL 00-D-40012 started its life as Dublin Bus AV12. The photo shows a line-up of Volvos on O'Connell Street.

Delivered as new to Dualway, this is Wrightbus Gemini 2 Volvo B9TL 151-D-26628.

GrayLine operates the Malahide Castle & Coastal Tour using Dualway Wrightbus Gemini 2 Volvo B9TL 151-D-26628, which was rebranded from standard City Sightseeing livery.

Similar Dualway Wrightbus Gemini 2 Volvo B9TL 151-D-25981 passing the colourful Doyle's pub.

Dualway Wrightbus Gemini 2 Volvo B9TL 161-D-28005.

171-D-41645 is a Wrightbus Gemini 3 Volvo B5TL very similar in design to the open-top buses used by Lothian Buses in Edinburgh on its City Sightseeing service.

Wrightbus Volvo B5TL 181-KE-3872 reaches the end of its loop on the Red Tour. The bus only wore City Sightseeing Dublin livery for a short period.

181-KE-3872. There was a big change for city tours during 2019. An agreement was signed between Big Bus Tours and the Dualway Group to acquire the company's Dublin-based City Sightseeing tours, previously operated by Irish City Tours.

Big Bus Tours Wrightbus Volvo B5TL 181-KE-3872 about to cross the River Liffey in the centre of Dublin.

Big Bus Tours Wrightbus Volvo B5TL 171-D-41645 showing off its new livery.

Another recent repaint into Big Bus Tours livery is Wrightbus Gemini 2 Volvo B9TL 151-D-25981.

Big Bus Tours 00-D-70101 is former Dublin Bus Alexander ALX400 Volvo B7TL AV101.

Big Bus Tours former Dublin Bus Alexander ALX400 Volvo B7TL AV34 (00-D-40034).

Another vehicle purchased from the UK. Big Bus Tours Plaxton President-bodied Volvo B7TL 03-D-82126 was new to Go-Ahead London as PVL356 (PJ53 NJZ).

Ashbourne Connect operates this very attractive liveried ADL Enviro400 MMC, 182-D-23470 (new as an ASDL demonstrator bus registered YX68 UPY), on the Dublin Brewery and Distillery Tour which completes the Golden Triangle, made up of the Guinness Stonehouse, Pearse Lyons Distillery, Jamieson Distillery and Teeling Distillery. (Noel O'Rawe)

AEC Routemaster 67-KE-16003, formerly RML2623 (NML 623E), in one of the distinctive Dublin Cityscape liveries. Cityscape operated a range of vehicles, allowing a new way to see all the sights of Dublin in all weather conditions. Tours were suspended in 2018.

Plaxton President Dennis Trident 2 708 (03-KE-16292), screened up for Kilmainham Jail. The bus was new to Metroline in London as TP380 (LR52 KWY).

Plaxton President Dennis Trident 2 702 (03-KE-16278), formerly Metroline TP392 (LR52 KXL).

Plaxton President Dennis Trident 2 701 (03-KE-16277), formerly Metroline TP385 (LR52 KXD).

Ei (Extreme Ireland) Travel Group now provides the City Sightseeing-branded franchise tours of Dublin using some former CityScape vehicles. 03-D-121607 is an Alexander Dennis-bodied Volvo B7L.

ZV 10903 – formerly London AEC Routemaster 811 (WLT 811) – runs on the Vintage Tea Tour, which allows passengers to enjoy afternoon tea delicacies, good conversation and 1950s jazz.

Dublin Bus Demonstrators

DM1 (14-D-19194) was a Volvo B5TL/Wrightbus demonstrator bus used to familiarise drivers with the new B5TLs Dublin Bus would be getting that year. In fact, Dublin Bus got 621 of them (but has subsequently lost an amount to Go-Ahead Ireland). It is seen on the route 9 from Charlestown (Finglas) to Limekiln in Walkinstown in June 2014. (Darren Hall)

DM1 is seen on Ballymun Road on service 9 to Limekiln Park in June 2014. (Darren Hall)

DM1 is seen at the route 9 terminus at Limekiln park in Walkinstown in June 2014. (Darren Hall)

DM1 on Griffith Avenue, the longest tree-lined avenue in Ireland, en route to Charlestown. (Darren Hall)

DM2 heading back to Foxborough in Lucan and passing the Customs House in January 2015. (Darren Hall)

DM2 (14-D-21502), a 2014 Volvo B5LH/Wrightbus seen in January 2015 on route 151, which it operated whilst in service with Dublin Bus. It had a reputation for being a troublesome bus. It is seen outside the Customs House, heading to the Dublin Docklands. (Darren Hall)

Trial of Dublin Bus Hybrids

Nine diesel-electric hybrid vehicles were introduced during 2019 as part of a plan by the National Transport Authority (NTA) to reduce carbon emissions. Painted in a bright green and yellow version of the company livery, the vehicles have low-floor access, dedicated wheelchair space and USB charging ports. VH3 (192-D-16983) is one of three Wright Gemini 3-bodied Volvo B5LHs in service and was pictured at Dennison's, Ballyclare. (Noel O'Rawe)

Another view of VH3 (192-D-16983) at Broadstone Depot prior to it entering service. At the time of preparation of this book, Wrightbus sadly went into administration and the future of its skilled staff and products, including any more builds for Dublin Bus, was unknown. It had been planned to put a procurement process in place for some 600 double-deck hybrid buses over a five-year period, with the majority in use in the Dublin area. (Darren Hall)

Wrightbus StreetDeck HEV96 WH1 (191-D-33234) is based at the Conyngham Road depot and is seen on service 25 to Merrion Square, crossing the River Liffey at Chapelizod. (Darren Hall)

WH1 (191-D-33234) leaving Aston Quay on service 25 to Dodsboro. These hybrid vehicles do not need to be re-charged using plug-in connections. Each are integral with a Daimler engine. (Noel O'Rawe)

In this photo WH1 (191-D-33234) appears at Nassau Street on its regular route 25 to Merrion Square. In the Government's plan for responding to climate disruption, it is envisaged that 1,200 electric buses will be in operation by 2030. (Noel O'Rawe)

One of the other three Wrightbus StreetDeck HEV96s WH2 (191-D-33233) is seen crossing the River Liffey at Heuston station on a 25 service to Dodsboro. The powertrain on board these buses can deliver fuel savings of at least 30 per cent, producing less CO_2 and helping to improve air quality. (Darren Hall)

The Alexander Dennis Enviro400H MMC Class is also taking part in the Dublin Bus hybrid trials. AH1 (191-D-44403) was the last to enter service and was photographed on service 25B to Adamstown station. (Noel O'Rawe)

AH2 (191-D-44404) is seen operating the 25D to Merrion Square on its first day in service. While similar in looks to the original batch of Enviro400s, the trial vehicles boast a more modern look and feature full-height upper-deck windows. These vehicles are the first Alexander products received since 2008. (Darren Hall)

Another view of AH2 (191-D-44404) in Adamstown, Lucan, County Dublin, picking up its first fare-paying passenger on the 25D to Merrion Square. The livery adapts the current yellow with two-tone greens, which possibly represent the colours worn on the fleet in the past. (Darren Hall)

A rear photograph of AH3 (191-D-44405) showing the lettering explaining that the hybrid bus is eco-friendly with lower emissions. (Noel O'Rawe)

Go-Ahead in Ireland

During 2017, the Go-Ahead bus group, based in the UK, won a contract to operate twenty-four Dublin Bus routes, which made up about 10 per cent of the city fleet. A brand-new route, the 175 service commenced in September 2018, with a number of existing Dublin Bus routes being acquired together with more new services starting over the following months. Mercedes-Benz Citaro O.530 03-D-121520 is seen promoting the new company and advertising for people to 'Join the Go-Ahead driving team'. (Alistair Train)

The original two-tone blue Go-Ahead livery, which was later to be changed to incorporate yellow, is seen at Bray rail station on 11508 (former Dublin Bus Wright Eclipse Gemini 3-bodied Volvo B5TL SG46) (142-D-15770) during driver training. (Noel O'Rawe)

More than 150,000 people travelled to Dublin in August 2018 to catch a glimpse of Pope Francis on his papal visit to Ireland. A number of park and ride hubs were set up to facilitate the crowds. Newly painted into the short-lived two-tone blue livery is Go-Ahead Wright Gemini 3-bodied Volvo B5TL 11557 (182-D-466) on a papal shuttle in Phibsboro. It would transfer people to Dublin Port, where coaches from the country were stationed for the duration of that day. (Darren Hall)

Undertaking driver training duties in University College Dublin bus park is Go-Ahead Wright Gemini 3-bodied Volvo B5TL 11573 (182-D-482). (Noel O'Rawe)

A newly built Wright-bodied Streetlite appeared at the 2018 Euro Bus Expo in Birmingham, showing off the final version of the Go-Ahead Ireland and Transport for Ireland (TFI) logo.

Go-Ahead Wright Streetlite 12105 (182-D-17892) in Dun Laoghaire on service 111 to Dalkey, which switched to Go-Ahead operation on 21 October 2018.

An unidentified freshly painted Go-Ahead Wright Gemini was captured heading along the A8 at Kilwaughter just outside Larne, Co. Antrim, while on a road test. (Noel O'Rawe)

Pictured while waiting time at the rear of Dun Laoghaire train station, this is Go-Ahead Wright Gemini 11576 (191-D-16296).

Go-Ahead Wright Gemini 11911 (132-D-11603) departs from Marine Road in Dun Laoghaire on the 45A to Kilmacanogue.

Pictured in the extensive and scenic grounds of University College Dublin is Go-Ahead Wright Gemini 11538 (17D-D-16283) on the 17 service to Blackrock DART Station.

A line-up of Go-Ahead Wright Geminis at the busy University College Dublin bus station. Go-Ahead Ireland operates from depots in Ballymount and Naas with a fleet of 140 buses at the time of writing. Some were formerly with Dublin Bus and others were delivered as new to the company.

Go-Ahead Wright Gemini 11565 (182-D-474) is seen climbing out of the coastal suburb of Dun Laoghaire on route 59 to Killiney Hill.

The 17 group of services is now part of the Go-Ahead operation. Pictured leaving the University College Dublin complex, this is Go-Ahead Wright Gemini 11503 (142-D-12042) 17 en route to Rialto.

Go-Ahead Wright Gemini 11092 (132-D-1725) leaves Dun Laoghaire on the 75 to Tallaght, a route that deviates from the original Dublin Bus 75 to take in Dundrum Luas Interchange and Dundrum Main Street.

Go-Ahead Wright Gemini 11588 191-D-41383 took part in the Bus Driver of the Year 2019 competition in Blackpool and is seen with a dramatic sea background. (Andrew Chambers)

Another view of Go-Ahead Wright Gemini 11588 (191-D-41383) competing in the Bus Driver of the Year 2019 competition in Blackpool. (Andrew Chambers)

An unidentified ADL-bodied Enviro 200 for Go-Ahead in Ireland leaves the ADL factory in Falkirk, Scotland, in September 2019. (Thomas McReynolds)

The same ADL-bodied Enviro 200 undertaking local road trials in Falkirk before delivery to Go-Ahead in Ireland in September 2019. (Thomas McReynolds)

Dublin Airport Buses

Former Go-Ahead London Wright Gemini 03-D-120673 (formerly WVL 124 (LX53 AZT)) on Premier Inn shuttle duties at Dublin Airport. (Alistair Train)

Aircoach operates a bus shuttle to the long-term parking areas at Dublin Airport using bendi buses such as this Mercedes-Benz Citaro Artic (09-D-5303). (Alistair Train)

Wedding Buses

Above and below: Dublin Bus has operated a variety of buses in a white-based livery used in public service but available for wedding hires. AV384 (04-D-20384) is seen operating the service 15C to Whitechurch.